Life in the Early Thirties

WHEN GRANDPA
WORE KNICKERS

FERN BROWN *and* ANDRÉE VILAS GRABE

Illustrated by JOE LASKER

ALBERT WHITMAN & COMPANY, CHICAGO

Text ©1966 by Albert Whitman & Company; Illustrations ©1966 by Joe Lasker
L.C. Catalog Card Number 66-16076
Published simultaneously in Canada by George J. McLeod, Ltd., Toronto
Lithographed in the U.S.A.

When we were your age
there were hard times in our country.
Most people didn't have much money,
and Father was lucky if he had work.
Still, everyone was in the same boat
so we made the best of things.
But our world seemed very new and up-to-date
to us when we were young.
Doesn't your world seem that way to you?
Yet your children will probably think how
old-fashioned it was when you were little.

At home and around the house there was
always plenty to do.

We ran errands, peeled potatoes,
    ironed handkerchiefs, set the table,
        dried the dishes, swept the walks,
            and practiced the piano.

What we liked to do at home was to
    draw a hopscotch game on the sidewalk,
        fly kites, jump rope, climb trees,
            play "Run, Sheep, Run,"
                and bounce a ball to O'Leary.

We had large kitchens with pantries,
and round wooden tables covered with oilcloth.
You would probably think that our kitchens
were not very bright because we didn't have
as many lights then—one seemed enough.
There was no chrome furniture or formica.
Mother's pots and pans were mostly iron,
and heavy as could be.
If they had special handles, you didn't
burn yourself—but if they didn't, look out!

In winter there wasn't a thermostat
to control the heat
so you FROZE.

You slept on a cold sleeping porch
or in an unheated bedroom
so you FROZE.

The bathroom didn't have a heater
so you FROZE.

The best way to keep warm at night was to sleep
with a hot-water bottle on your icy feet.

Oh, how good something like an electric blanket
would have felt.

We didn't have a vacuum cleaner,
　　an automatic washer and dryer,
　　　　a garbage disposal, a dishwasher,
　　　　　　an electric can opener or a mixer.
In fact, our homes had very few electrical appliances.

Mother used a carpet sweeper and dust mop.
We would beg her to let us take the dust mop out
and shake it very hard over the railing
and watch the dust
　　　　　　　trail
　　　　　　　way
　　　　　　　down
　　　　　　　into the alley.

When Mother wanted to clean the rugs, she would
roll them up (they weren't wall-to-wall),
hang them outside on the clothesline, and
　　　BEAT and BEAT and BEAT!

Some of our neighbors had washing machines, but our clothes were scrubbed on a washboard that had little metal ridges, washed in a tub, and then put through a wringer.

Mother had to turn the wringer with one hand and push the clothes through with the other to squeeze the water out.

In the summer, she hung the clothes outdoors on lines held up by poles. She dried them in the basement in the winter. Sometimes it would take two days for everything to dry. So Mother would bring the clothes upstairs to hurry them dry on the radiators.

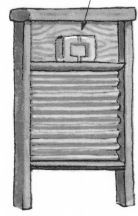

yellow laundry soap

a scrub board

But the worst was when it rained in summer, and all the clothes were hung out. Then we'd run outside to help take everything in. The radiators weren't hot, so we would light the stove and dry the clothes near the oven.

If only Mother could have had an automatic washer and dryer!

The BAKER, the BUTCHER, the GROCER,
  the dairy, the fish market, the candy shop—
    and not a SUPERMARKET in the lot!

We had a store for everything, and nothing
came in packages. We went out shopping
almost every day. Mother canned and preserved
most of our fruits and vegetables. A nickel
bought a pound of cooking apples, and butter
was 37¢ a pound. A family of four could
eat a good dinner for less than a dollar.

Do you know what store was the best of all?
The candy store! How we loved penny candy!
There were red licorice whips and black ones,
and little wax bottles filled with sweet juice.
After you drank the juice, you could chew
the wax until it was soft and stuck to your
teeth. We ate pink-and-white sugar candies
on a strip of paper. You just peeled them off,
one at a time—were they ever good! We ate
Mary Janes, chocolate soldiers, Tootsie Rolls,
and candy bananas and jawbreakers.
Nothing cost more than a penny—and
some wonderful things were TWO for a penny!

Mother had no mixes, no frozen foods,
no TV dinners, no "instant" anything.
Flour and sugar came in sacks, rice in barrels,
potatoes in burlap bags, butter in wooden tubs.
Chicken, chops, and steak came all-of-a-piece,
and fish were live! The man would wrap the fish
in newspaper, and you ran home with it and put it
in a tub of water. You had to keep the fish alive
or it would spoil.

We had no freezer, and most of us didn't have
a refrigerator—only an icebox.
The icebox had a large pan under it to catch
the dripping water. If you forgot to empty it,
it would overflow and maybe leak
through the floor, over the people downstairs.

The iceman came every other day. We would put
our sign in the window or at the back door
telling how much ice we wanted.
Five or ten or twenty-five pounds.
All the children would rush to the ice wagon.
It was a kind of covered wagon, pulled by a horse—
not like the wagon pioneers had—but with a heavy,
oily canvas top. Inside it was cold and dark and wet.

The iceman would take a large pick, chop out
our piece, then grab it with his big metal tongs.
He'd sling it on his shoulder and bring it
into the house. We children waited
for the iceman to come back. His horse
would stand quietly while we fed him carrots
or sugar. Sometimes we could only pet him
because he'd have his feed bag. We hoped
the iceman would hurry back and give us
little chips of ice to suck. He was nice that way.

Mother didn't buy our clothes for style.
She would always ask "How long will this last?"
Our things had to last a long, long time.
A brand new dress for Mother cost $5,
Father's suit was $15 or $20, and
his shoes $4 to $6. Doesn't that seem cheap?

We didn't have zippers. Such a little thing!
But imagine if you didn't have zippers
in all the places where you do have zippers!

Little boys wore sailor suits,
and bigger boys wore knickers to school
until they got to be about twelve years old.
Your first pair of long pants really meant
something. It meant you were a man.

Boys didn't care about clothes any more
than they do now, but they did like caps
and flashy neckties and argyle sweaters
with matching socks.

Girls *never* wore jeans or shorts,
just dresses or jumpers or skirts.
Dresses buttoned down the back,
jumpers buttoned on the shoulders,
skirts buttoned to blouses, and—
they all had snaps or hooks at the waist.

Girls loved clothes as much as they do now.
Little girls wore their skirts short so that
their matching bloomers showed. They loved
ruffles and bertha collars and big straw hats
with long ribbons fluttering down the back.

For gym, girls wore something
simply *spectacular*: great big black billowing
bloomers with middy blouses.
You could really do great stunts
in that outfit!

side view

Wool was for everything.   In winter we wore
wool underwear and wool stockings,
    wool sweaters and wool dresses,
        wool knickers and wool shirts,
            wool coats and caps and gloves.

When we were little, we wore woolen snowsuits
that Mother or Grandmother knitted for us.
The snow would cake hard on them
in great patchy chunks, and we'd look like
raggedy snowmen.

And in the summer we wore
    one-piece wool bathing suits
        or two-piece wool suits with belts.
The suits always stretched and always scratched
and always smelled woolly when they got wet.

We didn't have nylon or dacron or orlon
or anything drip-dry or wash 'n wear.
We wore cottons, voiles, dimities, and ginghams.
Mother starched our clothes so that they stood
as stiff as cardboard. Instead of crinkling,
they'd bend. You'd always have a sore neck
where your collar rubbed.

What kind of good times did we have?
Movies were fun because the movie stars
talked out loud. Talking pictures were still
something pretty new—we called them "talkies."
We paid 5¢ or 10¢ for the movie and saw
a stage show, too. It only cost an older person 25¢
if he went early.

On Saturday afternoons there were serials.
They were the most exciting of all, and if
we wanted to find out what happened to the girl
on the edge of the cliff or if the saw
cut the man in half, we had to come next week.
Do you think we could miss a single week?

Radio was so new we couldn't even imagine
television. It seemed wonderful enough
to turn on the radio and listen to news and jokes
and plays and music. Earphones were old-fashioned—
you could hear the radio anywhere in the room.

We called our record players phonographs,
and played records one at a time.
We were always having bad luck with records
because there were no unbreakable ones.

We took pictures with box cameras—sometimes
we called them Brownies. The film was all
black and white. We waited for big events
like graduations, weddings, or a new baby.
We didn't have colored film then.

Everyone was doing jigsaw puzzles.
Grandmother, Grandfather, Father, Mother—
even the tiniest children were doing jigsaws.
Some puzzles had hundreds of pieces.
You spread them out on the table after dinner
and everyone would help put them together.

When we said TOYS
we didn't right away think *plastic*.
Toys for babies were made of wood. There were
wooden pull toys, wooden beads, and wooden
blocks. And the paint would always come off,
especially if the baby chewed it.

We older children loved stuffed toys and
Teddy bears. But Mother couldn't wash our toys,
and they'd get so dirty that at last we weren't
allowed to take them to bed.

Of course girls had dolls and doll buggies.
If you made a doll bend over, it cried Ma-ma,
but that's all it would say.
Girls liked to have doll dresses to match
their own dresses. Mother would find pieces
of material and help with the sewing.
Our sewing machine wasn't electric. You put
your feet on the treadle and pushed them
        up and down, UP and DOWN,
and if your feet stopped, so did the machine.

Boys played baseball and marbles,
rode their bikes, spun tops,
and collected baseball cards.
Some of the big players every boy wanted
to collect were Babe Ruth, Gabby Hartnett,
Hank Greenberg, and Lou Gehrig.

Roller skates were fun, but stilts were
something special. We could stand up high
and walk around the neighborhood with
             L...O...N...G steps.
It didn't matter if you were the smallest
on the whole block, with stilts
you were even taller than a giant!

In the winter we would coast
down the hills on our sleds.
We didn't have disks to go 'round and 'round,
but we made our own funny ways. We would
lie on our stomachs or go down backwards.
If you were a real daredevil, you would
stand up all the way to the bottom.

We waited for the ponds and creeks to freeze
so we could slide and ice skate. We even
skated on lakes and rivers when they were
frozen solid.

When we were sick
  Mother usually had enough medicine
    in the house to cure us.
Sometimes she gave us terrible-tasting
castor oil or hot chamomile tea. You had to
hold your nose while it went down.
If you had a cold, she rubbed your chest with
camphorated oil or tried a mustard plaster.
Ouch! that hurt when Mother peeled it off.
And the hot milk and honey she made us drink,
when we coughed, tasted so bad that we'd
rather cough than have Mother's medicine.

If Mother couldn't cure us, the doctor came.
Our doctor wasn't "for children only."
He took care of Mother, Father, all of us,
even Grandmother.

We weren't afraid when he came to our house
because he smiled a lot and called us by our names.
He let us peek into his little black case.
There were millions of pills in it, or at least
a thousand. There were big pills of all colors,
and little pills of all colors, too. And bottles,
all shapes. Our doctor had the pills you needed
right in his black case.

The doctor didn't ask if we took our vitamins
because nobody had multiple-vitamin pills.
Maybe he'd tell Mother to give us cod-liver oil
or ask "Did you drink your milk?" or
"Have you eaten your spinach?"
The reason he never gave us sulfa or penicillin
or any antibiotics was because they hadn't been
discovered yet.

Tonsils came out in bunches.
You went to the hospital
with your brothers and sisters
and sometimes even some cousins.
It was great fun on the way in,
sort of a holiday.
But it was no fun the next day
when you couldn't swallow even ice cream.
That part hasn't changed much, has it?

Going to the dentist was a good thing to
try to get out of, if you could.
But if you had a toothache, you went.
The dentist didn't have novocaine.
He said he didn't mean to hurt us,
and he would give us a sucker or
peppermint stick afterward.

teacher wanted us
to sit like this
all day .... but mostly we sat like this.

seat
folded up

gum
(strictly forbidden)

READING 'n WRITING 'n 'RITHMETIC
    and history, geography, and English
        were our subjects.

Our school was called grammar school.
We had no social studies or science or
foreign language, but we had spelling.
We had manual training or sewing and
cooking, too.

We didn't have to learn as much as you do.
We didn't even have to know as many states.
We didn't study atoms and we never heard
of astronauts, but we sang a lot, songs like
"America the Beautiful" and
"My Country, 'Tis of Thee," and of course
"The Star Spangled Banner."

Sometimes we had forty-eight children in a room.
Everybody sat in the same class and had
the same teacher for every subject
and did the same work at the same time.
Our desks were piggyback and nailed to the floor.
There was an inkwell in each desk, and a boy
would fill the inkwell from a big bottle of ink.

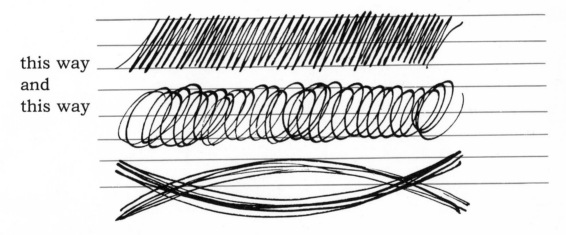

↙ teeth marks

You put a pen point into a penholder and dipped
the pen in the inkwell and practiced penmanship.
Every day you practiced writing—

this way
and
this way

push, pull, push, pull.
It was called the Palmer Method, and we thought
that it was the only way to write.

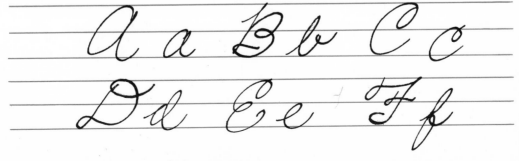

CLEANLINESS IS NEXT TO GODLINESS

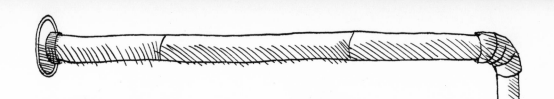

Did you ever hear of portables?
They were separate schoolrooms that could be
moved to different places, something like
trailer homes you see today.
When the regular school building was crowded
and there was no money to build a new school,
we went to class in portables. They were
lined up like tin soldiers on the playground.
The wooden boards between them made a sort of
wooden sidewalk for us to walk on.

We had a sign in our room saying
"Co-operation is the Spirit of Portable 19,"
and another, "A soft voice denotes culture."
We tried to keep our portable just as nice
as the rooms in the big building.
We even took the curtains home for Mother
to wash.

There was a coal stove in the back of our room.
It was a great place to dry mittens, but if
you put rubber boots there—look out!
Sometimes they got so hot the room smelled
of rubber. If you sat near the stove you got
hot and sleepy. But if you sat near the windows,
you froze. That was how it was in portables.

We had no extra teachers, except for music.
Teacher ran the class
   and teacher ruled the class
      and a mother *never* came to school
         unless a child had done something very bad.
Sometimes if you were ahead of the others, you
skipped a grade. That meant you were pretty smart.

We never talked much about going to college.
We thought that anybody who graduated
from high school was an educated person.
A lot of boys and girls had to quit school
to go to work.

Many kids in the upper grades had jobs
after school. A boy was mighty lucky if
he earned $3 a week in a grocery store,
putting circulars in mailboxes, selling papers,
or shoveling snow. The money always
went to Mother to help out at home.

When the telephone rang
we ran to answer it.
We had stand-up phones,
and crank-up phones in some places.
If your family had a party line, you could
listen to what a neighbor was saying, but
you weren't supposed to. Some homes had
nickel phones, like those in public booths.
A man came around to collect the money.

Our phones didn't have dials or push buttons.
You'd pick up the receiver and the Operator
would say, "Number, ple-uz?"
And you'd say, "Give me Idlewood 2375."
Now we have numbers—at least seven of them—
and an area code, too. What do they think we are,
IBM machines?

the operator

a stand-up
phone

The postman came to our house twice a day,
morning and afternoon.
He'd ring our bell and we'd dash to see
if there were letters for us. We loved to send
for free things advertised in magazines—
toothpaste samples and cereals, booklets
on child care and recipes.

If we mailed a letter to someone in the
same city we lived in, it only cost 2¢.
A letter sent anywhere in the United States
was 3¢. A government postcard was only 1¢,
and we called them penny postals.

Telegrams were for bad news.
If you were handed that dreaded yellow envelope
you'd be afraid to have someone open it.
Of course, sometimes it was good news.
"The new baby's name is Thomas. Everyone is
fine. Love, Uncle George." The message had
ten words and then the signature.

Automobiles were beginning
to be important in our lives.
One lady told a newspaperman she'd rather
have a car than a bathtub.
Why? "Because you can't go to town
in a bathtub!"
That's how important everyone thought
it was to own a car.

But lots of roads weren't paved,
and they were not well lighted at night.
It was no fun to be out after dark.

Short trips took a long time.
A trip that takes a half hour now
took an hour and a half when we were little.
Can you guess why cars didn't go very fast?
They weren't built that way. A speed of
45 miles an hour was about the very best
a car could do, but most of the time
Father didn't drive that fast.

We had trouble with our cars. Very often
we'd have a loud BLOWOUT. Then the tire
had to be changed, and we'd hope we wouldn't
have another blowout for at least a few days.
And sometimes the car ran out of gas.

Do you think there was a gas station on every corner? No—sometimes there wasn't a gas station for miles around.

But it was still wonderful to have a car because you could drive out into the country on Sunday, to the woods or to the beach.

Cars didn't have
    electric windows and turn signals,
        power steering and air-conditioning,
            tubeless tires and shatterproof glass,
                sealed-beam headlights and radios.
And there were no hardtop convertibles.

gas pumps

station wagon

But there were ROADSTERS and RUMBLE SEATS and RUNNING BOARDS.

Rumble seats were wonderful open-air seats behind the covered ones. Mostly the children sat in the rumble seats because mothers didn't like to have their hair blown. You stepped on a step at the bumper, then you climbed on the fender where there was another little step—and then you jumped into the seat.

When no one sat in the rumble seat, you closed it. Presto! No seat!

Running boards were on both sides of the car. Cars were built high off the ground, and you had to step on the running board to get in. You didn't bump your head because car roofs were higher then. Mother wore her hat with a tall feather and didn't worry about spoiling it.

rumble seat

running board

convertible roadster

Streetcars were for people
who didn't have cars.
You could ride a streetcar
    downtown, to work, to school,
        to the beach, to the park,
            and even to a picnic.
Sometimes if you didn't have anything to do
you could always ride the streetcar
from one end of the line to the other and back.
The neighborhoods went whizzing by, and
you could watch the writing on the store windows
change from one language to another.

Every streetcar had a motorman in uniform
who sat on a little stool at the front of the car.
He made the gong go CLANG! CLANG!
to tell everyone to get out of his way.

There was a conductor on the rear platform
to take your money. He called "Fares, please!"
and "Step lively!"

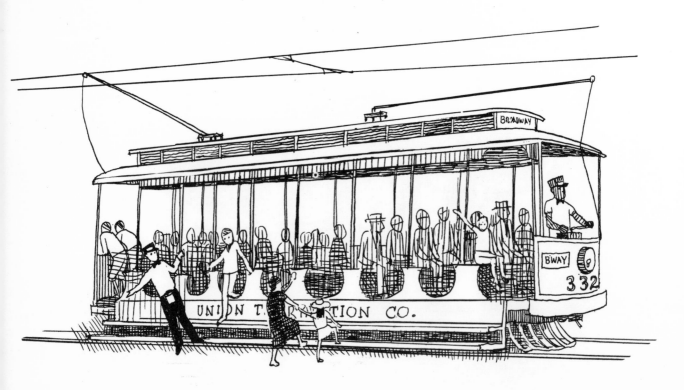

The conductor had a coin changer on his belt.
Maybe the fare was 7¢ for an adult and just 3¢
for a child. When everyone was on, the conductor
would signal the motorman by pulling a cord
that rang a bell at the front of the car,
DING! DING! That meant "Go ahead."
There'd be a loud H'sss as the long trolley pole
glided along the overhead wires and the car
would sway from side to side.

We sat on reed-covered seats and looked out
through the mesh that was supposed to keep us
from putting our hands out the windows.
In the winter, the windows were steamy,
and we rubbed places to see through.

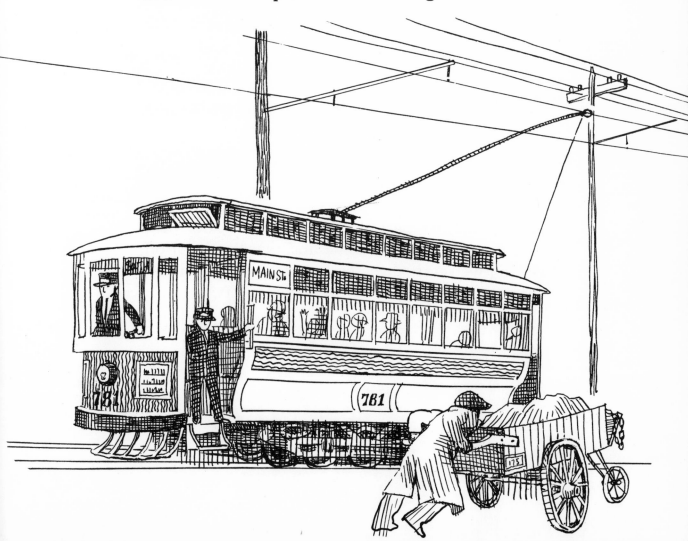

Trains were for long vacations and
visiting far-away relatives.
The conductor put down a little stool,
and you climbed into the train and hurried
to pick out the best seat—they weren't reserved.
Those beautiful green plush seats looked
like velvet, but sometimes they were scratchy.
Four seats faced each other on each side
of the aisle. We chose the ones that faced
backwards.

There were dining cars, but most of us
brought food along because it was too expensive
to eat all your meals in the diner.

The big steam locomotive huffed and puffed.
It made long stops to get water and fuel.
We could get off and watch the men work
and sometimes buy apples from vendors.
But when the conductor shouted "All ABOARD!"
we ran because we didn't want to be left behind.
The train wouldn't wait for anybody!

The conductor checked our tickets.
If we were going far, our tickets
might be over a foot long.
Every time we passed a city named on our ticket,
the conductor would come and tear that part off.
When we reached the end of our trip, we didn't
have even one teeny scrap of ticket left.

Our trains were hot because there wasn't any
air-conditioning. When we were tired of sitting,
we'd beg Mother and Father to let us visit
the observation car.

It was hard to push the doors open, and the train
swayed from side to side. Gusts of wind
blew across you as you tried to get to the next car,
but it was worth it to get to the observation
platform. It was something like a little porch
right at the end of the train. You could sit
on a folding chair and wave to people you passed.

Night was the best time on the train.
Then the pullman porter would come to make up
the beds. Sometimes he'd tell stories or do
tricks while he worked.

Remember the two seats that faced each other?
The porter pulled them into the middle and
their backs came down to make a bed.
That was the bottom berth.

But we children loved to climb the ladder
to the top berth. Even though it didn't have
a window, it was the best place to sleep.
The porter put a crank in the sloping train
ceiling. Then he unfolded two dividers
and pushed them into place. He pulled down
the top berth, and there were two mattresses,
four pillows, sheets, and blankets for the top
and bottom berths. And do you know what else?
A long green net hammock to string
from one end to the other of the berth.

When you were ready to undress, you pulled
the green curtains in front of the berth shut
and buttoned them. Then you scrunched yourself
together to get undressed. You put your clothes
into the hammock when you had your nightclothes on.

There were washrooms at the ends of the cars,
one for ladies and one for gentlemen. Going down
the aisle, you tried not to bump anyone
or step on somebody's feet.

Airplanes were new and exciting to us.
Just think—men had flown across the oceans
and around the world!
Children didn't go up in planes very often.
Flying was mostly for men who traveled on business
or for daring people with lots of money.
But we liked to visit the airport and watch
the planes take off. How fast the propellers
whirled! When a plane came in, we held our breath
and watched it swoop down, down,
and we didn't breathe until it had landed
safely. Then we counted the passengers,
maybe as many as ten.

• • • • •

We enjoyed our growing-up years,
and sometimes we wish for the "good old days"
when we were your age.
Then we tell ourselves that we haven't left
anything behind, we've only replaced it
with something new.
Maybe you'll say the same thing someday!